# How to teach this unit

By year 3/4, children's observation is becoming more sophisticated. They have definite views, likes and dislikes; they notice discrepancies and try to find explanations – sometimes arriving at the wrong conclusions! The time is ripe for you to help them develop their observation and enquiry skills, and link them to an understanding and appreciation of the built environment. These concepts link easily with sustainability and citizenship – see http://www.livingstreets.org.uk/

It might be imagined that an investigation of 'our street', being so familiar, might be commonplace and dull. In fact, the reverse is the case, as the popularity of soaps based on the lives of people in their local area proves. Neighbours, Coronation Street, East Enders and Hollyoaks all illustrate the dramatic appeal of familiar contexts – the interplay of the geographical elements of work, play, everyday living, citizenship, conservation and the sustainability of purpose of the neighbourhood. How did their street become as it is? Who lived here? Who lives here now? Are there any blue plaques? What is there up the side streets? What are the back gardens like? What is underneath the street? How could we improve our street? Understanding the cultural, historical and geographical factors which have resulted in the unique character of their street will create a sense of ownership and responsibility for their environment: active citizenship.

## Time allocation

The teaching time available for geography can vary enormously. SuperSchemes units have been written with three possibilities in mind:

- a **short–medium** unit (5–10 hours)
- a **long** unit (10–15 hours)
- a **continuous** unit (15–30 minutes per week).

The medium term plans allow you to choose an appropriate length for your particular class. Some of the longer medium term plans offer enough material for you to continue with the topic later in the year.

## What do I need to know?

Every place has a distinctive character. Where is the street going to/coming from? Roman streets went on for hundreds of miles; see if your street ever has been, or still is, part of a longer route. Can you find it on the oldest OS and earlier maps? How old is your street? If it is in the middle of an estate with crescents and closes, it's probably modern. If you can find long-held connections to other places, you are probably in the part of town which grew out along the main roads in the late 19th and early 20th century. If you are in a curvy street layout, then you are probably in part of the estate development and infill that characterise the second half of the 20th century. What about the character of the buildings? Are they built of honey-coloured stone or bright red bricks? Do they have timber cladding or fanciful decorations round the windows? How is the land used in the gardens, the yards, the shopping areas and along the side streets? Are you in the centre of a town, or on the edge – the rural–urban fringe? In either case, there are good reasons for aspiring to maintain and improve the distinctive character of your street.

## Subject knowledge

Asking questions about the location and character of the street helps us understand how buildings reflect the period when they were built and their original use. Over time these features may have changed to accommodate the changing geography of the street and its local area. For example, spacious Victorian houses built for large families have often been converted into a number of flats: external stairs and a row of bell pushes are evidence of this change. Former stables and carriage houses alongside or behind the original dwelling, often reached through archways, have been converted to garages and workshops. Gardens and stable yards have often been built over by extensions to the original building. Older rows of shops near town centres may have been converted from houses: flat-roofed extensions where front gardens used to be give these away. Small developments of new houses on main roads may reflect small petrol stations that have gone out of business! Most primary schools are in suburban areas, but ever-increasing road traffic can be a problem for some schools: what may have been a quiet, leafy lane is now a 'rat run' for commuters. The main concepts and the implications for learning are shown in the table below.

# Key ideas

## Geographical concepts related to locality knowledge

| Questions | Concepts | Knowledge |
|---|---|---|
| What is a (any) street like? | Streets reveal the activities which maintain everyday life. They have distinct places and buildings for meetings, rest, exchanging goods and leisure. | Understanding the location of distinctive features, and the space requirements for different land uses<br><br>Map and photograph interpretation skills |
| Where is our street? | Different places have both similar and unique features.<br><br>Differences in landscape can be natural or manmade. | The location of the street within the physical and human features of the local area<br><br>Its geographical growth, and changes due to historical events<br><br>Atlas, map and photograph skills; research and descriptive skills |
| What is this place like? | Buildings reveal how towns have grown. The oldest houses are usually nearest to town centres.<br><br>Each building period has distinctive street patterns and house designs related to the physical character and original land use. | Recognition of the age and use of buildings<br><br>Observation and recording skills<br><br>Making maps and recording changes<br><br>Checking these against historical maps and documents |
| What do people do here? | Buildings and land along the street are used differently at different times, e.g. during the day, in the evening, at night, during the week, and at weekends and public holidays. | Comparing a range of building ages and character over time<br><br>Comparing land use for leisure, services and shops<br><br>Measuring and making maps, and using enquiry skills to create a database |
| Where do people go from here? | Commercial and leisure activities are often close together and away from residential streets. Community and leisure provision, often variable, is not always visible.<br><br>Parks and open areas fulfil several roles and should be part of the regeneration and sustainability plans of any neighbourhood. | The location of work and leisure activities in the home area; the various networks connecting such activities<br><br>Characteristics of urban and rural parks; the use of nature trails and green corridors<br><br>Map and photograph skills, role play and enquiry skills |
| How did this place get to be like it is? How is it changing? | Streets change in character over time.<br><br>Change of use relates to change in the location of activities, and can create tension through conflicting interests. | Factors affecting the growth of the street, e.g. transport routes, availability of building land, and expansion or contraction of work opportunities<br><br>Use of historical maps, photographs and documents at local and national level |
| How is the environment managed? Why do some landscapes need protection? | Different human activities create different environments.<br><br>Grants, subsidies and controls are management activities initiated by groups.<br><br>Individuals have responsibilities for conservation and sustainability. | Knowledge of community and national moves for conservation and sustainability; Local Agenda 21 activity<br><br>Map and photograph skills for reportage<br><br>Developing evaluation skills to research the local area for change and improvement<br><br>Role play for different viewpoints in relation to particular projects |

## References

DfEE/QCA (1998/2000) *A Scheme of Work for Key Stages 1 and 2.* London: DfEE/QCA.

# Where do I start?

Starting from children's own knowledge and experience, the unit:

- encourages children to record street features, using camera, tape recorder, map and pencil
- shows children how to trace development over time, using old maps, directories, newspapers and census documents
- develops children's observation and recording skills in considering environmental likes and dislikes, visual improvements and responsibilities, and numerical and literary associations
- fosters enquiry skills, by comparing maps of different dates, building geographies of the street inhabitants and their occupations over time
- extends children's knowledge of their own street through fieldwork and research.

## The importance of progression

Children may have carried out work on the local area during key stage 1, and they will almost certainly do more of this later on. This means you need to ensure that they are challenged and stimulated throughout. It may also necessitate the creation of a school plan for work in the local area throughout the primary years, and this could even form a creative and useful basis for initiating discussions with secondary schools.

The street you study could be the one in which the school is situated, or a street where some of the pupils live. You could start with a residential street, and move on to one offering more amenities.

## Safety issues and risk assessment

A local enquiry field trip will make the work interesting and attractive. Make sure you follow school or LEA guidelines on safety and adult–pupil ratios. Once you have completed a risk assessment, it will only need updating before each trip.

## Preparing for a trip

Before the children start out on a local enquiry, you need to prepare them for the trip on the school site, developing their observation and recording skills, as well as self-management using clipboards, drawing materials, etc.

## Collect resources

Resources about the local area will support enquiry work in the classroom, and will be relatively easy to collect. Suitable resources might include:

- a range of local maps, including historical maps, and local history booklets
- photographs and a digital camera for children to take their own photographs
- local newspapers
- names of people willing to talk about living in the area
- contact details for local societies and parish/district councils
- local census material
- local development plans and information on important local issues.

## Preparing yourself for the trip

- Walk round the school's local area with friend and note not only the landmarks but also specific changes in houses, gardens – and places to stop safely. Take photographs.
- Collect photographs, both past and present, by using your local history library (past geography).
- Whilst at the local history collection obtain information about who lived in the streets you are visiting. You can find these in, for example, old copies of *Kelly's Directory* as well as census returns.
- Visit the web to collect maps at different scales (e.g. Multimap, Get-a-map) and of different ages (e.g. Oldmaps) with the current aerial photographs to match.

## Preparing the children

- Set up an 'explorer's competition' for who can locate the most interesting garden/building/sounds on their way to school.
- Look at the school grounds for the children to map their likes and dislikes (affective mapping) and then, with the aid if possible of disposable cameras, extend to making posters of children's favourite places in their neighbourhood.
- Discuss the essentials for a 'good' neighbourhood and use them to develop the key questions (page 7).

# Concept map

**OUR STREET**

- Is it easy to tell?
- What is the age of the buildings?
- How 'green' is the street?
- How are they different / similar?
- What are the houses like?
  - Is the street a safe place?
  - Are there any derelict buildings?
- Are there any open spaces?
  - Where do children play?
  - Are there any leisure facilities?
- How is the street changing?
  - How might it look in the future?
- Is there any street furniture?
  - What type of signs are there?
    - Are there too many?
- How can you travel to and from the street?
  - Is parking an issue?
- Are there buildings other than homes?
  - What are they used for?
    - Did any well-known people live here?

# Medium term plan: Our street

| Learning outcomes | Key questions | Pupil activities | Resources/ Key vocabulary | Assessment opportunities |
|---|---|---|---|---|
| To develop a sense of place<br>To ask geographical questions<br>To use geographical vocabulary<br>To use secondary sources<br>To identify physical and human features<br>To identify patterns and processes | What is our street like?<br>What is it like to live in our street?<br>What are the main features in our street? | **1** Ask each child to write down/draw/describe what their street is like, what they like/dislike about it. Talk about what they think about the street: has anyone lived anywhere else, and how does it compare?<br>**2** Discuss what buildings are made of (**activity sheet 1**).<br>**3** Prepare children for visiting the chosen street (see **lesson plan**). | Aerial photos of school/home locality<br>Large-scale map of local area<br>**Activity sheets 1, 2 and 4 and Resource sheets 3a and b**<br>*town, village, settlement, street, road, homes, shops, services, factory, buildings, transport, land use, environment, repair, damage, pollution* | Can the pupils describe their street using geographical terms? |
| To observe, collect and record information<br>To analyse information and draw conclusions<br>To be able to describe what places are like<br>To use appropriate geographical language<br>To carry out fieldwork<br>To use appropriate ICT | What is this place like?<br>What is it like to live in this place?<br>What are the buildings used for?<br>What materials are used in the buildings in these streets?<br>What do people do in our street?<br>What facilities are available in the street? | **4** Conduct a fieldwork visit to the street. Observe and sketch buildings, record street furniture, and note down building materials and styles. Try dating buildings. Were there any people, traffic, etc.?<br>**5** On your return, collate the findings and present them using ICT, e.g. graphs/charts. Consider the jobs that people in the streets do.<br>**6 Further work.** How do people travel? Investigate the transport network for reaching the street. Are there any issues relating to travel? | Fieldwork equipment: clipboards, recording equipment, digital cameras, video recorders<br>*street, road, close, land use, environment, repair, damage, pollution, community, signs, derelict, converted, Victorian, Edwardian, modern, terraced, detached, semi-detached*<br>**Activity sheet 2** and **resource sheet 3** could be used during this field trip | Can the children give a presentation (oral or written) describing the features of the street they visited? |
| To analyse information and draw conclusions<br>To use appropriate geographical language<br>To identify and explain different views<br>To communicate in different ways<br>To identify patterns and processes | What is changing in our street?<br>Can you remember any changes in our street?<br>Who could we ask?<br>What could change in the future? | **7** Look at an early OS map and compare this with a recent map. What has changed? Record your findings. Use **activity sheet 5**. | Old OS maps<br>Local newspapers<br>Access to planning documents<br>*change, homes, shops, roads, services, environment, repair, damage, pollution, community, derelict, future* | Can the children describe how the street has changed? Do they think these changes are for the better? |
| To express views and opinions<br>To communicate in different ways<br>To analyse information and draw conclusions<br>To use appropriate geographical language | How can we improve our street?<br>What would you like to see changing in our street?<br>What might other people like changed? | **8** Revisit the work that was done at the start of the unit when the children were asked what they thought they would see in their street.<br>Ask them to draw or write about what their street might look like in the future and why things have changed. | *street, road, change, homes, shops, roads, services, factory, buildings, transport, land use, environment, repair, damage, pollution, community, derelict* | Can the children to draw or write about what their street might look like in the future?<br>Can they justify the changes they have recorded? |

**Cross-curricular links:**
**Literacy** – speaking and listening (interviewing), writing reports, poetry (writing impressions of our street), fiction (creating stories about families in our street), **ICT** – databases and graphs, **History** – changes in people and places over time, **Citizenship** – being members of a community, **Art and design** – building a collage of buildings in our street from observation and photos, **Maths** – handling data.

# Lesson plan: What will our street be like?

**Subject:** Geography (year 5-6)

**Time/Duration:** one hour

## Learning outcomes

In this lesson children will learn:

- to use geographical vocabulary and fieldwork techniques and equipment
- to collect and record evidence and ask questions
- to identify and describe what places are like.

## Background to the current lesson

Children will already have looked at maps and aerial photographs of the street and talked about their likes and dislikes of features in streets they know. NB This lesson is designed to be taught before a field visit to the street. The initial choice of street might be in a residential area, followed by a street with more amenities.

## Lesson details

### Introduction

Having divided the class into mixed ability groups, ask them to discuss and record what materials they think they might find in a street. How might the buildings vary? Bring the class back together and share these ideas. (5 minutes)

Ask the children to think about what features buildings will share, e.g. roof, walls, etc. Give the children **activity sheet 1** (on CD) and ask them to complete this in pairs. Bring the class together and go over their answers. (15 minutes)

### Main activity

Tell the children about the visit you are all going to make to a named street to look at it in more detail. In pairs again, ask them to predict and write down on a sheet of paper what they think they might find. What sorts of buildings will they see? How old will they be? Will there be any shops or services there? What will they hear or feel in the street? How far away are other places (shops, transport links, etc.)? Discuss their predictions as a class and display them so they can revisit them on their return. (15 minutes)

Explain to the children that they will be making a field visit to a nearby street in the next lesson. Go over any health and safety issues that need to be addressed, and show the children any equipment that they will be using, as well as any recording sheets that will be used. (15 minutes) (**NB** Remember that you must have performed a risk assessment of the area to be visited before the visit takes place.)

Share with the children the activities you will ask them to do (e.g. **activity sheet 2**) and give them copies of **resource sheet 3**, which will help them to date the buildings.

### Plenary

As a homework activity, the children could be given **activity sheet 4** and asked to look at either their own or a nearby house and record the details asked for. Make sure that all the children understand the terminology on the sheet. (10 minutes) (Their returned sheets can be displayed afterwards around a map of the area.)

## Differentiation

The children should be arranged in mixed ability groups for this lesson. The class teacher and another available adult should support individual groups as necessary.

## Resources

Large sheets of paper and pens for each group

Activity/resource sheets 1, 2, 3 and 4

Fieldwork equipment and outline maps of the area to be visited.

## Cross-curricular links

- **literacy** – speaking and listening
- **citizenship** and **PSHE**
- **science** – materials
- **history** – local history.

# Further ideas for developing this unit

Display the pictures of various types of street furniture from the CD, and ask the children questions about them – for example:

- What do the signs mean?
- Where do you find them?
- Are they informative or instructive?
- Where do you find these signs in our area/my street?
- Can we find examples in our area where there seem to be too many signs in one place?

Investigating a street will inevitably involve both geographical and historical aspects. The children can be asked to carry out research about individual buildings and homes going back in time:

- Who lived there?
- What jobs did they do?
- What was the building used for?
- How has it changed?

Old newspapers, personal accounts, census returns and old pictures will provide useful resources. The children can develop a story involving some of the characters or events they have discovered.

Create a collage of a particular street either in the present day or in the past.

Investigate houses in your local area by cutting out a range of adverts from the property section of your local paper. Give the children a set of pictures – for example, **resource sheet 3** – and ask them to group all the examples they have from the paper. Which age of housing is most/least in evidence?

Ask the children to think about the future of a particular street:

- What changes are happening?
- What might this street look like in 50/100 years' time?

Use homework opportunities to ask the children to make observations/drawings/collect information about their own street. Display these around a large-scale map of the area and discuss their findings.

Encourage the children to make a Powerpoint presentation about their street/area for presenting to a number of visitors to the area. What would be interesting and informative to others?

Give the children a drawing of a street with several blank spaces between the buildings. Ask them to create suitable houses/buildings to fill the spaces. They will need to think about the design of the buildings on either side of their proposed one, and be able to justify their choice of age and style of buildings.

In a chosen street, identify all the ways in which parking is controlled. Ask the children to list these and form an opinion about the success or otherwise of each method. Why do they think they have been introduced? (A suitable street for this exercise might include some of the following: time limited parking, a ban on parking, parking notices, yellow/red lines, parking meters, traffic wardens etc.)

In a residential street where the houses tend to be uniform in style, for example on a housing estate, ask the children to record the different ways in which people attempt to make their house distinctive. These may take the form of structural features, such as different materials or facings for driveways, garages and external walls or more personal touches such as flower baskets, different doors or name plaques. Discuss why people make these changes. What effect do they have on a neighbourhood?

Consider what can be done now to improve the street aesthetically and sustainably, e.g. where could space be used to grow vegetables as well as flowers and trees? Use a slogan such as 'Plant to save our climate' (see http://www.livingstreets.org.uk/).

Relate your observations of the different uses of the street to the rest of the settlement. Consider potential changes for other parts of the town – and begin preparation for looking at 'Our Town'.

# Using the activities

## Activity sheet 1: Parts of a house

This activity reviews previous learning and ensures that the children understand the correct terminology for the different parts of a house. It can be printed off as an activity sheet or transferred to the IWB to serve as a class revision activity. You will need to emphasise to the children that this is just one type of house – a Victorian villa – and that other houses may have some but not all of these features. It will be helpful to discuss how houses built at different times show additional features: for example houses built in the 20th century may have garages, patios, gardens or conservatories. An annotated version of the house illustration can be found on the CD.

## Activity sheet 2: A street survey – building use

This can form the basis for observation during the field visit. The information can be complemented by a drawing or a photograph, and will make a good addition to the classroom display. The individual data collected by the children can be collated into a land use database. This will be an important resource: it constitutes an historical record which can be used for future work on the street, allowing children to identify changes over a span of time within their experience.

## Resource sheet 3: Telling the age of a house

This will be a useful sheet for reference when the children are out on a visit. The pictures can also be used as a strip, with house pictures cut from local newspapers displayed alongside. A good discussion point will be the authenticity or otherwise of features characteristic of a particular historical period. Are all buildings with Tudor features really Elizabethan? How can we tell the difference between real Tudor and mock Tudor?

## Activity sheet 4: Age and style survey

This is a starter activity to help children develop their skills in drawing houses with the help of a key. It can be used when they are out on a visit, and will be especially helpful for less-able pupils. It may also be useful as a homework exercise, providing a range of information from across your area that will contribute to an informative display.

## Activity sheet 5: Changes to houses

This activity encourages children to look very closely at individual buildings to identify change. Children find careful, close observation a difficult skill to learn, and one way to help them practise this technique is to start by displaying a close-up of a house on the IWB and encouraging discussion. Houses which look very similar at first sight may actually exhibit significant differences when examined carefully: replacement doors and windows, rear extensions, attic dormers, etc. A further option might be for them to talk to the people who live in the houses about changes over time. Such an exercise will prove both valuable and interesting for the children, but you will need to arrange this beforehand. At the same time as asking permission for the children to ask questions, it is useful to prime the adults with the type of questions the children will ask and the type of replies they will find helpful.

## Display the activities

Pull together the collected information using a blown up copy of a colour map or aerial view of the street upon or around which the photographs and drawings can be located. Give meaning to the idea of change by putting a timeline beneath the map to link with relevant places displayed on the map above. Local visitor(s) could well have photographs to support this idea.

# Activity sheet 1: Parts of a house

Name _____

Use the word bank below to help you put names in the boxes for the different features of this large house. Not every feature has a box.

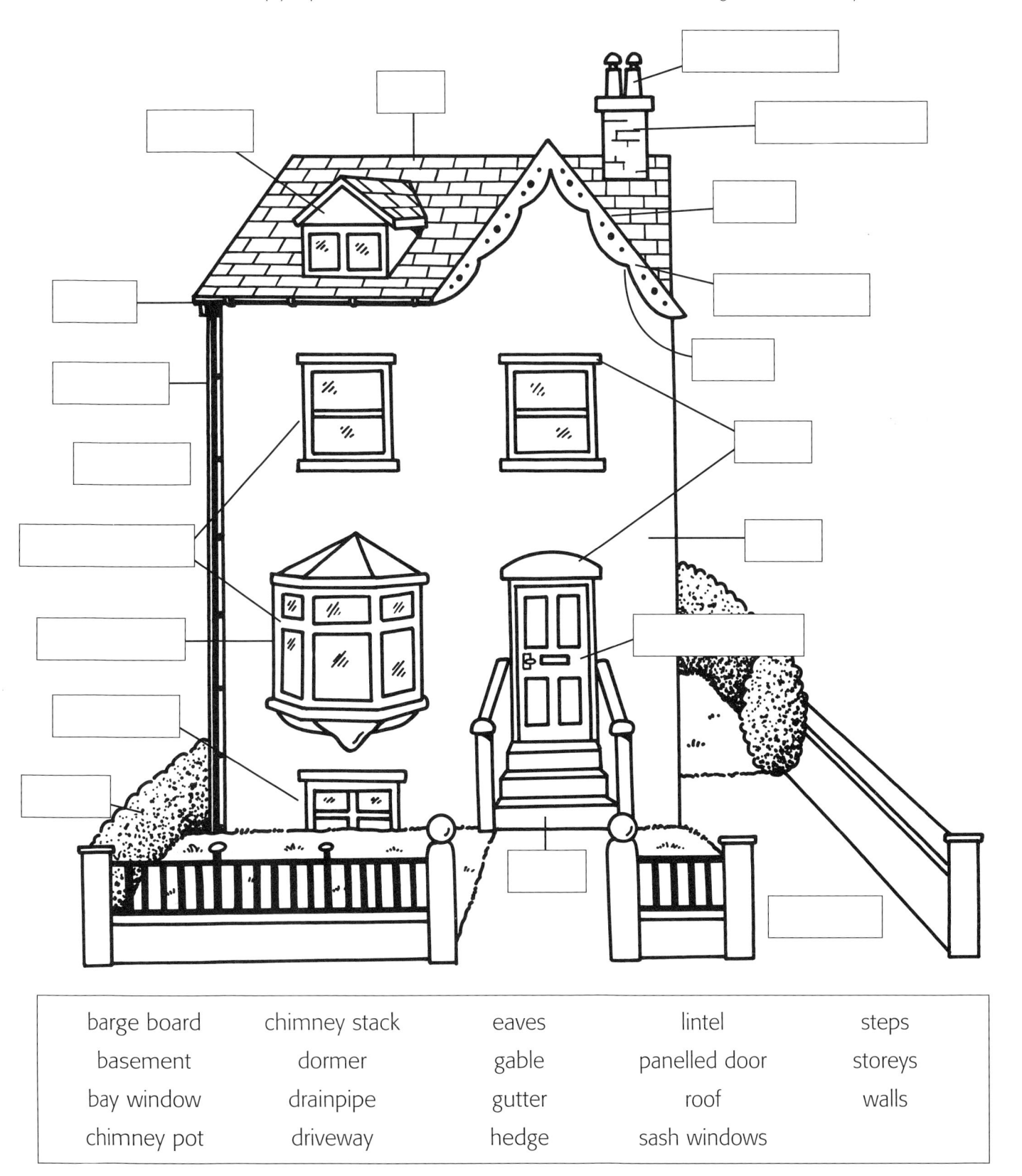

| barge board | chimney stack | eaves | lintel | steps |
| basement | dormer | gable | panelled door | storeys |
| bay window | drainpipe | gutter | roof | walls |
| chimney pot | driveway | hedge | sash windows | |

Think about the different houses in your area. Do all houses have these features?

**Investigating the local area: Our street** *by Rachel Bowles*

This unit uses enquiry skills from geography, history and art to look at 'any street' as a useful pre-requisite to looking at 'any town'. The main purpose is to develop curiosity and an eye for detail, and so widen children's knowledge and understanding of familiar and unfamiliar places. The evidence gleaned from close observation helps children to understand about maintaining historical character, developing a good quality of life and the role of citizenship in the environment. Children will develop a sense of responsibility towards the built environment, and learn to appreciate the cultural, historical and geographical factors which have led to each street having its own character.

At the same time, they will develop detective skills – observing, noticing discrepancies, finding explanations. Who lived here? Are there blue plaques? Who lives here now? What is up the side street or in the back garden? What can we do to improve our street? This is a chance for children to engage in active geography and make practical contributions to the life of their own neighbourhood.

Rachel Bowles is co-ordinator of the Register of Research in Primary Geography and an Honorary Research Associate of the University of Greenwich.

---

© Geographical Association, 2005

This book is copyright under the Berne Convention. All rights are reserved. Apart from any fair dealing for the purpose of private study, research, criticism or review, as permitted under the Copyright, Designs and Patents Act 1988, no part of this publication may be reproduced, stored in a retrieval system, or transmitted in any form or by any means, electronic, electrical, chemical, mechanical, optical, photocopying, recording or otherwise, without the prior written permission of the copyright owner. Enquiries should be addressed to the Geographical Association. As a benefit of membership GA members may reproduce material for their own internal school/departmental use, provided that the GA holds copyright. The views expressed in this publication are those of the author and do not necessarily represent those of the Geographical Association.

ISBN 1 84377 139 X

First published 2005

Impression number 10 9 8 7 6 5 4 3 2 1

Year   2008   2007   2006

Published by the **Geographical Association**
160 Solly Street, Sheffield S1 4BF.
The Geographical Association is a registered charity: no 313129.

Design concept: **Bryan Ledgard**
Design: **Ledgard Jepson Ltd**
Copy editing: **Asgard Publishing Services**
Maps: **Paul Coles**
Illustrations: **Linzi Henry**
Acknowledgements and photo credits can be found on the CD
Printed and bound in England by Henry Ling Ltd, The Dorset Press

### SuperSchemes

Each unit in the SuperSchemes series comprises a booklet, a CD and a regularly updated website area:

Unit 1   Around our school: The seagulls' busy day *Colin Bridge*
Unit 2   Making our area safer: The twins on holiday *Colin Bridge*
Unit 3   An island home *Liz Lewis*
Unit 4   Seaside selections *John Halocha and Vanessa Richards*
Unit 5   The world comes to Barnaby Bear! *Elaine Jackson*
Unit 6   **Investigating the local area: Our street** *Rachel Bowles*
Unit 7   Hot, cold, wet, dry? *Margaret Mackintosh*
Unit 8   Improving the environment: Access for all *Simon Catling*
Unit 9   Village settlers *Paula Richardson and Emma Till*
Unit 10  A village in India *Jo Price*
Unit 11  Water *Pam Copeland and Des Bowden*
Unit 12  Looking at Europe *Paula Richardson and Emma Till*
Unit 13  A contrasting UK locality: Where do you want to go today? *Paula Owens*
Unit 14  Investigating rivers *Andrew Turney*
Unit 15  The mountain environment *Tony Richardson*
Unit 16  What's in the news? *Kate Russell*
Unit 17  Global Eye *Tony Richardson*
Unit 18  Connections: Integrating ICT into geography *Wendy Garner and Tony Pickford*
Unit 19  Where we go, what we do *Margaret Mackintosh*
Unit 20  Geography and culture *Emma Till*
Unit 21  Improving the view from our window *Sue Parsons*
Unit 22  A contrasting overseas locality: The Gambia *Pam Copeland and Des Bowden*
Unit 23  Investigating coasts *Tony Pickford*
Unit 24  Passport to the world *Larraine Poulter*
Unit 25  Geography and numbers *Paul Baker*
Unit 26  Investigating the local area: Our town *Rachel Bowles*

**The Geographical Association, 160 Solly Street, Sheffield S1 4BF**
tel 0114 296 0088    fax 0114 296 7176
www.geography.org.uk    www.geographyshop.org.uk

ISBN 1-84377-139-X
9 781843 771395